The Joy
of Being
BROKE

The Book for
people who
would Be Rich
if they just had
More Money

Ben Goode

Published by:
Apricot Press
Box 98
Nephi, Utah
84648

books@apricotpress.com
www.apricotpress.com

ISBN 1-885027-41-2

Illustrated & Designed by David Mecham
Printed in the United States of America

Introduction

We picked up some cereal at the store the other day and noticed two things right away. First, the boxes were much smaller than we remembered from a week ago when we bought the same cereal; and second, the amount of air in the boxes was just a little greater relative to the cereal in the boxes than we remembered from last time. Being the financial gurus we are, we thought, "What a great idea!" In these tough times, unless you're the government, the health industry, or one of the businesses being bailed out by the government, you need to cut every possible cost just to survive. And just like the cereal manufacturers who didn't cut quality (the actual sugar content of each morsel was as decadent as ever) we don't want to cut quality either.

So in the spirit of trying to stay competitive in good-old competitive free-market America, and trying to survive in these tough times, we are going ahead with publishing this book--but we are printing it with 25% fewer words. Hopefully the economy will turn around soon and we can afford to go back to printing as many words in our books as before. However, regardless what the future brings, with Apricot Press, the quality will always be there; you can count on that. If things get so tough we get down to only one word in our books, you can bet that word will be a really, really good one. And for now, the 75% of the words left in the book will be extraordinarily funny to compensate for the slight drop in content. Thank you.

-Ben Goode

Contents

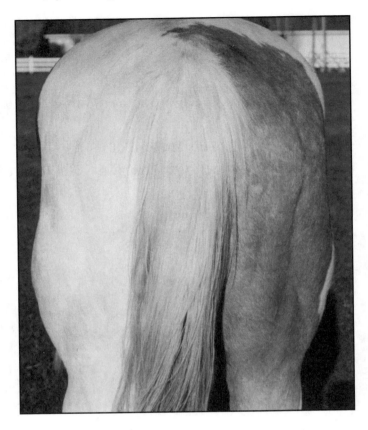

"A wise banker once told me that the sole
reason they charge $24 for a bounced check
is out of concern for their customer's
character - to teach them to manage their
money better. Really! I think he was
serious! I acted like I was sucking it up
because I really needed the loan."

1

Joy Through Poverty

Maybe you're a person who is already broke. Maybe you're just sick and tired of being wealthy and successful and you're ready to try something else for a while, like poverty. Maybe you're just a bumbling incompetent, one of the economic fire hydrants living in this worldwide financial dog kennel who always seems to be in over his head. Maybe you're one of those people for whom it seems that every time you stick your little lice-infested gopher head out of the hole for some economic fresh air (metaphorically speaking) some economic game-playing big shot pounds you down with his financial mallet. How would I know? You're the one reading the book. But whatever your reasons, I know this book is for you. It will give you perspective.

It will give you relief. It might even give you the hives if you rub it on your pet before you read it.

The Dawn of a New Day

For all of human existence it's been the rich and powerful who are often also mean and nasty, along with the obnoxious, aggressive and pushy who always get to call the shots. This is not fair. There are lots more poor, incompetent, wimpy, self-defecating, nice people being walked on than there are rich, obnoxious bullies who brazenly use the rest of us as their personal economic jogging track. Since when do we let a small, vocal, obnoxious, misguided minority impose its will and values on us?

OK. That was a stupid question. Of course I realize that my thesis sentence in the above paragraph was, in essence, that the rich and powerful always get to call the shots. Sorry. Of course I am aware that the majority of us spend pretty much our entire lives allowing an irritating minority to impose its will on us. I am a journalist. Of course I know that a clique of self-appointed social bullies decides that we have to pay $200.00 for sun glasses, show our underwear over the tops of our pants, get tattooed, and be embarrassed to be patriotic or religious. Yes, I have been clued in that a small, militant, angry group of food Nazis is, without our permission, switching our diets from yummy steaks, potato chips, and bacon and eggs to tofu and Brussels sprouts. Sorry for bringing up such a painful subject, but my point is it's time to take back the planet for the unfortunate, the incompetent, the fearful, the indolent and dense, the shortsighted, the whiney, and the narcissistic. There are lots more of us than there are people who are rich and competent. If we common folk stick together, I'll bet there's nothing they can do about it, at least the sticking together part. We have pitchforks and torches. Let's take back the world for the lazy and incompetent. We can do it! The French pulled this off a couple of centuries ago and look how cool they've become.

All we have to do is come up with a way to do it. I'm sure I could come up with some ideas for how to take back the planet, but of course they would all cost some money. So, what I'm looking for is somebody who is poor, pathetic, and obviously not too bright, who also happens to have a big pile of money which he or she would be willing to donate to a worthy cause. When I find someone like that, I can go to work fixing this problem. Here's how I propose we make it happen: First, we need to get Ben Goode elected president. That will give me access to all the money in the world, since I will be the C.E. O. of the printing company.

Next, since pretty much every special interest group in the country would be opposed to me on both sides of the political aisle, we won't have to worry about using any of our money and power to take care of our friends like the other political parties since we aren't likely to have any friends. Since everybody will hate us already, we can go to work bailing out all the people who have been left out of the last few rounds of political partisanship. I will promise right here that if you will vote for me, I will give each of you a million dollars and you don't even have to win a reality game show to get it. Just give me a call, and if you are pathetic, and can prove that you voted for Ben Goode, you get the money. I don't care at all what you do with it. I hope you spend it very unwisely. You just have to promise to go right out and spend it fast in order to stimulate the economy. If I gave out stimulus checks like this to a million of my friends that would only be one lousy trillion dollars, if I got my arithmetic right. And if I'm wrong and I'm off a couple of decimal points, so what. We can make all the money we want to.

Since this first proposal is about as likely to happen as the environmental big shots are likely to sell their palatial estates and gas-guzzling private planes and cars, or my goat, Ernie, is likely to stop eating my mulberry tree, or as likely as your pickup truck is to start producing its own gas from the fast-food wrappers on the floor in the front seat, we probably should be looking for some other way to find happiness other than success and wealth. Let's give it a try.

The Way to Success and Happiness Other Than Wealth and Success

Of course the world has known for centuries, and most of us at least suspect that wealth, power and success don't buy happiness. Since it's also well known that sleep and chocolate trifle often do, it seems that we should concentrate on those things that are known to work and forget about money, since somebody already got that avenue locked up.

In my family it has long been known that one of the keys to joy and happiness is adequate sleep. Since many of you have made this discovery as well, here is some little known information about sleep that I have accumulated over the years that you may find useful:

Some little known facts about Sleep that will Give You Happiness

1. While you are asleep, it is impossible to be doing a whole bunch of the things you hate to be doing such as getting spattered with hot grease while cooking burgers at the Tasty Freeze or roto-rooting out Mrs. Wilkinson's clogged toilet.

2. While you are asleep and dreaming about that hot babe or guy that is way beyond your reach socially and economically, it is physically impossible to be thinking about all your financial problems, therefore it stands to reason that you would be pretty happy at these moments.

3. If, while you are sleeping, a swarm of Huns, Vandals, terrorists, or Vikings should descend upon your house and kill you, since we are all going to die sometime anyway, and if most of us had a choice we would choose to die in our sleep, being killed while dreaming about hot guys or girls is probably one of the best ways to go.

There. We have proven that if you're sleeping if anything at all is actually happening it is most likely going to be a good thing, we recommend sleep as one of the great keys to happiness and success. Let other people worry about the money. We will deal with the chocolate trifle later, unless we forget.

It stinks to be
on the road.

"Nothing in life is certain except death
and taxes,,, and the car breaking down
whenever you get $300 saved up."

2 Same Things Are Worse Than Being Broke

For some people being broke is tough, especially if they are not used to it. If you happen to be a person who really struggles with being broke, having a healthy perspective can be helpful. So quit whining you sniveling boob and take a look at these things that are worse than being broke:

1. Being Sushi.

2. Having the earth's newest volcano erupt right underneath your car while stuck in traffic.

3. Being duct-taped to a communications satellite and shot into outer space in your underwear.

4. Finding out during your insurance physical that you have two appendix and no brain.

5. Finding out during an insurance physical that what you thought was a zit is really your microscopic friend, Ralph, building a swimming pool on your chin and you killed him with rubbing alcohol this morning.

6. Finding out during an insurance physical that you have absolutely no guts.

7. Drinking one last glass of whiskey after you know you shouldn't and waking up a few days later inside a coffin.

8. Being used as a pylon for a new pier.

9. Having a sorceress turn you into a cockroach because she's mad at you for some insensitive comment you made.

10. Having all your lumpy places sanded off with crushed glass.

11. Having really bad allergies and, after blowing your nose, finding a pound of plutonium in your Kleenex.

12. Finding a pound of brain matter in your Kleenex.

13. Finding the carcass of your schnauzer, Sparkey, who has been lost for a couple of weeks, in your Kleenex.

14. Finding your missing eyeball in your Kleenex.

15. Being a fishing worm or grub.

16. Waking up in Hell and finding you're surrounded by 13-year-olds with boom boxes.

17. Waking up in Hell and finding that you're buried up to your nostrils in bat guano.

18. Waking up in Hell to find that you will spend eternity watching reality TV. interspersed with political attack ads.

19. Waking up in Hell and finding that you're up to your chin in onion juice.

20. Finding that you're buried in Compound W.

21. Being a 900 pound steer ready for that last trip to the market.

22. Falling out of an airplane and grabbing onto the landing gear.

23. Having your dentist alternate using a 3/4 drill bit, a reciprocating saw, and a nail gun on your mouth.

24. Being a male black widow or praying mantis.

25. After sneaking over the fence into the swimming pool realizing that you and your buddies accidentally broke into a polar bear exhibit.

26. Hitting a cow on your Vespa at 40 M.P.H.

27. The cow wouldn't think this was very good either.

28. Discovering that the car you just stole belongs to a CIA operative code-named Fritz.

29. Waking up to discover that an elephant has paused to relax by sitting on your head.

30. Being buried up to your chin in fresh hippo dung.

31. Boarding a United Airlines flight to San Diego and discovering after a few hours that you accidentally wound up on the United Arab flight to Somalia.

32. Being forced to listen to political ads all year every year... wait! We already have to do this. Sorry.

33. Forgetting to feed your cat and being turned in by your animal rights enthusiast neighbor and being sentenced to death by political speech.

34. Forgetting to feed your cat and being sentenced to being pecked to death by hostile ducks.

35. Being buried up to your chin in scorpions and red ants.

36. Being licked to death by cats.

37. Strapping on a bunch of dynamite to go blow something up and stepping on a land mine on the way out of your bunker.

38. Waking up with a bad hangover at a Beastie Boys concert.

39. Having your car break down and spending a week in Bevis Falls, California and having to listen to the locals brag about the Lakers.

40. Having the Federal government run out of businesses to take over and having them nationalize your wallet.

41. Snorking back a big, cold bottle of green punch on a very hot day and realizing, just before you pass out, that it's antifreeze.

42. Being devastated because for 20 years you believed people have been buying your books because they thought you were funny, when in fact it's because they have secret love messages from Christine Aguilera hidden in the text.

43. Having to listen to political talk radio all day everyday.

44. Finding out the IRS has been secretly camped out in the attic monitoring your weekly bingo games.

45. Getting your denture adhesive mixed up with your grain fungus prescription.

"A group of congressmen
during a training exercise
at a weekend retreat."

Ben Goode

3

The Joy of Being Broke

Many, many, many people today are broke. Sadly, many of them are also bitter and cynical. I'm not. I can see much to be glad about in poverty. For starters, most of us really don't have much to worry about because the government is fixing everything. Happily, they are taking on the responsibility to make a bunch of us rich. To reassure us, for starters they have given all kinds of money to the banks. Even though I probably won't be getting any of this banking money because I already owe the banks quite a bit, you've got to be happy for all the bank employees. Before long, they're going to be rolling in it. If you divide a paltry five hundred billion dollars by the few thousand bank employees, the per-employee wad of money is more than most small

15

countries make in a year. I would actually tell you how much that is, but five-hundred-billion won't fit on my four-dollar calculator. Trust me. It's a lot of money. Congratulations bank employees and bankers on your futures of wealth.

I am also happy for the autoworkers. The government has given billions and billions to GM and Chrysler, too. Just a small chunk of even one measly billion divided among the few thousand autoworkers will have them all doing back flips. Lord knows they deserve it after all the crap they've been through over the years. Sadly, none of these billions will likely ever find their way to me either because it doesn't look like the automakers will be hiring old guys like me any time soon. (Apparently they wanted to divvy up their cut among themselves.) And they probably wouldn't hire old, arthritic guys anyway even as CEO.

I am also happy for all the people who work in the government because it looks like they are giving lots of money to themselves. I am happy because maybe now with all this money and power they are giving themselves they will finally be happy. (OK, I know, I know, the Republicans won't be happy for a while because nobody is giving them and their friends any money because they screwed everything up. Fortunately, there aren't too many of them any more so the whining shouldn't be too loud.) The Democrats, on the other hand, should be especially happy with all this money they are giving to themselves and their friends and they were so very, very, very unhappy for so long. Now that they are rich and powerful we can assume that they will be very, very happy and will stop complaining so loud.

I must confess that I never saw a Senator or Congressperson with a hole in his shoe or who had to take the bus to work because his Fiesta had a bad water pump and he couldn't afford to fix it, but I'm sure that given these times senators and congresspersons are struggling just like the rest of us. So now they have loads of money and therefore should be the happiest people we've ever seen.

If you add up all the banking people, all the auto people, and all the government people, that's a lot of people who will now be rich and happy. My friends and I have decided that seeing all these people so very, very happy will make us happy too, even though we are still broke. It's kind of like watching rich, beautiful people on TV. Watching how happy they are creates an escape for us so we don't have to think about all our problems for a while.

This leaves me and my friends. I must confess that we have been whining and complaining as loud and long as anybody else. Sadly, despite all our grumbling and complaining, so far none of the people passing out the billions seems to be taking notice of us. This is baffling because we can whine and complain like the dickens. In case anybody with billions is listening, we all agree that we don't need even billions. In fact, you could placate the whole bunch of us with one or two paltry millions. What would be the harm in that? No one would even miss it. You could attach it to a bill on global warming and nobody would even notice. Who reads those bills anyway? It seems we have been over-looked. Needless to say, we are trying to figure out a way to get a Senator's attention.

The Joy of Being Broke

Until that happens, we figure that if we're going to benefit from any of these bailouts, it's beginning to look like we're going to have to figure out how to do it by bailing each other out. Since I know there may be a few others like us in this same boat, I wrote this book mostly to get rich, but also hoping that those of us who get passed over when the government passes out billions of dollars will read this and feel better about being broke. Most likely we have to come up with our own answers. Fortunately, you have this book. I have come up with some solutions for those of us who didn't cause the problems, but who will most likely wind up paying for the solutions the government comes up with.

To start with, since this is all about change, I promise to start by changing my attitude. Instead of being stressed and frustrated about being broke, I, for one, am going to view my cup as half full. This should be easy since I have lost just about half of my previous income and half of my retirement. So, from now on, I am looking for happiness that can be found in losing money and being broke. Yes, I am taking happiness and joy from simple things like watching my toes wiggle through the sole of my shoe and the daily conversations with creditors, and from watching them nail those two or three corporate executives who stole all of the trillions of dollars and caused our country to go bad and hold congressional hearings while saying nasty things about each other and then go out and spend more of our kids and grandkids' money. We are going to work on our happiness by expanding our understanding about happiness and otherwise tossing a bunch of horse biscuits around.

A Few Secrets About Happiness

As mentioned before, we all know perfectly well that all those politicians and their friends who are right now rolling in dough, thinking they're going to be happy, are in for a rude surprise. We simple, incompetent, wretched, and unsuccessful people know perfectly well that no amount of money will buy them happiness. Are they ever going to be disappointed when they find out!

Let me see. In an earlier chapter I promised to talk about chocolate, which is one of those things that have been proven to buy happiness. I think this would be a good place.

A Few Secrets About Chocolate

1. For most of my life, I was told that chocolate makes you fat and causes zits. Fortunately for us, science, at least the kind paid for by the chocolate companies, has discovered that chocolate is good for you. This past year I have read numerous articles about the benefits of chocolate. Some even insist that it can cause you to lose weight. I'm guessing that the zit part of this was a lie by the anti chocolate lobby, too.

2. If your mouth is full of chocolate, you can't be eating red meat or pasta, which have been proven to cause obesity,

diabetes, heart disease, and many other related problems.

3. Since chocolate is often a comfort food, it stands to reason that while eating chocolate many people would consider themselves comfortable. Comfortable is the opposite of uncomfortable, which is similar to unhappy and miserable. Therefore, one can prove mathematically that chocolate eaters are less likely to be miserable or unhappy.

4. Many very good things are made from chocolate: eclairs, trifle, almond clusters, brownies, pies, and cakes, just to name a few items. Since good and bad are opposites, it can be proven mathematically that since these chocolate things are so good, it is impossible for them to also be bad.

5. Chocolate can be enjoyed by everyone regardless of social, political, religious, or economical status. There are the uber elite limited edition chocolates for the euro pinky waving aristocrats, the upper tier chocolates for the aspiring middle-class chocoholic, and the candy-coated chocolates for the rest of us

rednecks and trailer abiding folk.
Chocolate can be given as a gift or given
up for Lent. Christmas and Easter are
nearly dipped in chocolate each year and
are none the worse for it.

There. There are a few secrets about chocolate that
should make you happy being broke.

"Financial tip #864: Never tie
your dog up to a strange truck,
financially speaking."

4 How to Budget when You're Broke

Financial experts tell us that one of the reasons for financial failure is that many people fail to make a good budget and stick to it. Knowing our audience as we do, we suspect there may be a few of you out there reading this book who fall into this category. In a spirit of wanting to help, but knowing it's probably futile, we have prepared a sample budget from our vast experience in high finance. Here is a sample monthly budget you can use as a model if you want:

REVENUES:
1, Income from sale of plasma $112
2. Government Stimulus check   (Still waiting)
3. Income from sale of tools $118

4. Income from sale of watch	$20
5. Pawning neighbor's tools	$360
6. Pawning wife's jewelry	$245
7. Kiting bad check from one account to another	$200
8. Loose change from sofa	$2.16
TOTAL INCOME	**$1,057.16**

EXPENSES:

1. Redeeming wife's jewelry	$575
2. Abscessed tooth dental expense	$400
3. Bad water pump in '96 Fiesta	$850
4. Dog food	$22
5. Gas	$375
6. Bail-speeding ticket	$275
7. Loaf of bread-thrift store	$1
8. Arithmetic error in checkbook	$215
9. Bounced check charges	$80
TOTAL EXPENSES:	**$1,057.16**

Though experts tell us that a budget is important, the key to inner peace while being hounded by creditors, as we have found out is not to dwell on the budget for very long. The best way we can think of to do this is to join the Yanomamo in the Brazilian rain forest. However, while this may cure your preoccupation with your budget deficits, it may also get you killed by poisonous snakebites or eaten by piranha, so this solution may not work for some. As an alternative, many people and corporate accountants have come up with a strategy known as "creative math." Done correctly, this can be the consummate merger of the left-brain and the right-brain hemispheres. It stands to reason that the better your two brain hemispheres get along, the happier you will be, so this alternative strategy may just be your ticket to economic bliss.

The principles of creative math are simple and illustrated above in our sample budget. Principle number one used in depth by such corporate moral giants as Enron and Congress is to simply overstate revenues and understate expenses. The budding CPA can do this by inadvertently omitting a few expenses or by writing in the amounts wrong. The easiest way to do this is through creative use of decimals. For example, when the President and Congress want to make all the swing voters think they're cool and pick up the tab for everybody's prescription medication so they be sure and remember to vote for them next election, but they know darned good and well that one little phase of the program will cost say…two trillion dollars, if somebody in the general accounting office simply slides the decimal point a couple of slots to the left, all of a sudden an outrageously expensive program becomes almost embarrassingly affordable. You can do this with your own budget.

Let's say you have no money and your wife is complaining about being broke. You show her that you have two dollars and eighty-five cents of cash in your debit card. Using creative corporate, government accounting methods, in an instant, that can become two thousand eight hundred and fifty dollars and your wife is happy, at least until she goes to the mall and tries to use the debit card. So it's very important that you not think about or dwell on what may happen in the future because that will stress you out. Stress is not good.

Another thing that is not good and that we suggest you not dwell on is the idiotic things our politicians are doing, spending us into oblivion, because that will also stress you out, which can lead to heart attack, stroke, and armed revolution, none of which are good. So, unless you are prepared to go join the Yanomamo, we probably need to change the subject. We are going to illustrate how to do this to help those of you who don't know how. So for now, we're going to talk about my cell phone.

My Cell Phone

I am an older person. My cell phone is two-years-old, which in cell phone years is about a hundred-and-ten. I like my cell phone because I know how to use it. I know how to answer phone calls. I know how to make a call on it. This past year, my kids and grand kids even taught me how to receive and send a text message so I can communicate with them if they want to. Unfortunately, my 110-year-old phone is dying since I dropped it in the sprinkler. If I get a new one, I will have to re-wire my senior-citizen brain in order to answer it, make calls, or send messages. So I am thinking of getting a loincloth and joining the Yanomamo in the Brazilian rain forest so I don't have to deal with technology any longer...or budget.

The other problem I have is that I am not proficient in Farsi, Swahili, or any of the other 500 African, Asian, and Latin American languages that people who do tech support over the phone and help with tech problems speak these days. I figure that if I'm going to invest my few remaining years in learning a new language, I would prefer it was Yanomamo rather than East Indian because the Yanomamo have only a 300-word vocabulary, most of which refers to food. I can deal with that.

So, if you don't like to budget with no income, maybe you could consider joining me on my pilgrimage to the Brazilian rain forest.

"The Western Barn, long a safe place for animals, can also be a great place for you to hide out from re-po guys trying to pick up your quad ATV or from the tax man trying to re-po your moonshine still."

5 How to Get Rich

Sadly, despite my best efforts there will undoubtedly be a few of my readers who don't buy my blather about chocolate and sleep and other methods of being broke and happy. Some of you are going to persist in your futile efforts to become rich. Rather than lose you to other financial authors, we have decided to include a chapter about getting rich in this book in order to cover all our bases and make more money, which, although we know won't make us happy, at least we will be miserable with money.

How to Make Billions of Dollars with Little Effort and Zero Risk in Fifteen

Minutes or Less when All You Have as Resources are a few Friends Lying Around Your Apartment, Who are Also Broke, and Your Cell Phone Bills

Here's how you do it: Give me a thousand dollars and I'll tell you enough to get you into trouble. Then, if you send me some more money, I will let out a few more of my secrets. And then if you send me a whole bunch more money and then some more and then some more, I can gradually tell you the rest of my secrets-one-at-a-time, until ultimately you will know almost everything I do. And the nice things is, you can absolutely trust me. I would never ever ever try to get a whole bunch of people buying one thing in order to jack up the price because I bought positions in it earlier when it was a lot cheaper in order to jack the price up so that I could sell to suckers when it is over priced and make a killing. No, you can feel perfectly safe giving me you money because I would never do anything remotely like that.

Wealth has been coveted for many years—guys like Hernando Cortez, Ghengas Khan, political incumbents, and the BCS coalition have been willing to lie, cheat, kill, and even work in order to achieve fabulous wealth. And then, even more astounding, on top of that, guys like The Wiggles and Howard Stern are willing to become pigeonholed for life as complete idiots to get their pile of dough. So we see, that wealth must be one of those things that people seem to want almost as much as they want to finish a sneeze when they're right in the middle, and almost as much as they want other people to think they are cool, and so, after years of pondering the secrets of money and having my picture taken next to a Rolls Royce, I am finally feeling like an expert, like now I'm ready to reveal the secrets of fabulous wealth. And the amazing thing is I want to share them with anyone who will send me a thousand dollars.

Yes, in this fragile, uncertain world, the only sure way to get rich is to respond to an ad by someone who touts himself as an expert and then buy his book, go to his seminars and give him a bunch of your money. Then he will tell you his secrets and you can then use them to be rich like he did.

The thing that sets me apart from other money-grubbing promoters is that I am not motivated by money in the least. Yes, unlike so many other greedy, power hungry suede-shoed hucksters, I am pretty much a monk and only care about you and your success, which is why I am only charging $1,000 and not a hundred thousand for my secrets, and which is why, I myself am not rich. I am trying to save some for you.

I am willing to tell the whole world my secrets because I feel like the more the merrier. I don't know about you, but I would hate being the only rich person in the world. It seems to me that most normal people feel really uncomfortable around really rich people. So send me your money and we'll all get rich together and then there will be lots of us and nobody will need to feel uncomfortable.

Since I also happen to be the kind of guy who really wants to lose weight, but definitely not bad enough to stop eating sausage and eggs or to start exercising seri-ously, and who also wants to have the government do everything for me that I don't want to do, but then who thinks that they will do it all without wanting to control my life (and there must be a bunch of us out there) I knew it was time for me to write this chapter.

And who better to do it than me, since I am the only person I know who has never ever won anything and so, if I can get rich, I am going to have to take drastic measures. I'm going to try and get rich the old fash-ioned way-by holding get rich quick seminars and writing a book.

Since I figure there are lots of good people out there who don't forward the chain letters even when threat-ened with the Pharaoh's curse or eternal damnation, I figure if I'm going to get people to buy my books and pay money to attend my seminars, I'm going to have to crack some hard heads symbolically, to wade into some deep water, and maybe even come up with some plau-sible sounding secrets of wealth accumulation to pass onto my gullible readers.

Some Plausible Secrets of Wealth for my More Gullible Readers

Secret #1 • Send me a thousand dollars (or more if you want to). I know that this doesn't sound like that big of a secret, but it stands to reason that if nobody sends me money, I probably won't get very rich, and if you don't send me money, you will never know whether or not these secrets that I have will ever have worked for you.

Secret #2 • Send me a bunch more money to attend my seminars. Hey, this seems to be the universal formula for success that you see working everywhere. As I explained above, if you don't send me a bunch more money to attend my seminar, I obviously won't be getting very rich, in fact, we probably wouldn't even be holding seminars if nobody sends money, and you will never have the filthy lucre-making success secrets from my seminars and you will die wondering if that would have been the secret that would have made you rich as stink.

Secret #3 • After you have attended my seminars and read my book and found out whether or not these are the secrets to incredible wealth that will work for you, go back to your boring job, stay out of debt, and save money until you have enough to be rich.

*** *I plan to hold my first seminar as soon as I can afford a tent.*

"They say that in order to launch a big
financial ship, one must wade into
deep water. With your skills and experience, you should probably launch your
boats in the bathtub to avoid the kelp
and jellyfish."

6 Rich People Who are Wretched

All is not roses for rich people either. Things could be worse than being broke. Some people who are rich are captives to their money and fame. Some are slaves to it. Some are really weird. Quite a number of rich people are in such rough shape that they are actually dead. Here is a list of people who are rich who are also wretched. Surely you don't want to join this group.

1. Your lawyer

2. Howard Hughes

3. Your congressperson

4. Your Senator

5. Your drug dealer

6. Your drug-dealing congressperson or senator

7. Your proctologist

8. King Tut

9. The collection agents on your tail

10. Telemarketers

11. Telemarketing collection agents

12. King Nebecudnezzar

13. Michael Jackson

14. The Great Gatzby

15. Dale Carnegy

16. King Darius

17. Queen Victoria

18. Darth Vadar

Reasons to Feel Great About Being Broke

1. You are part of the largest peer group in the world.

2. Poverty can be used as a wonderful excuse for avoiding lots of unpleasant things: paying taxes, driving, picking up the tab, paying your bills, etc.

3. You have exactly the same amount of stomach bacteria as the successful, rich, and famous.

4. Trendy pants with holes and wrinkles make a fashion come back every few years.

5. If you had money you would probably just blow it anyway, then you would feel bad.

6. You can't drop a whole lot lower financially speaking at least.

7. When you are poor, you don't have to worry about being called greedy or selfish.

Wishing You Were Here

"Some of you may want to
send this postcard to your
accountant, stockbroker, banker,
or congressperson."

7 Saving Money on Everyday Things

When you are broke and pathetic you have to save money any way you can. Here are a whole slew of money saving tips anyone can do to slide by on little or no money so you can save up to pay your taxes or credit card interest and support the bail outs.

How to Save on Medical Bills

1. Since studies show that upwards of 50% of all doctor visits are unnecessary, if you're trying to save money, we recommend you only go to the doctor 50% of the time when you're sick. Be sure and select those times to go when you really need to, such as when, after three weeks your leg or head has failed to reattach after

being sewn back on, or when your fever is being used to heat the local city-county building complex or military base.

2. Do all the simple medicine yourself. You don't need to pay a surgeon to do simple procedures like wart removal, foot scraping, pre-cancerous skin spot removal, tonsillectomy, appendectomy, vasectomy or lobotomy.

3. Deliver your own children at home or better yet, when contractions start getting close have your husband drive around for a while at high speeds until you get pulled over by the police. Then you can have a policeman deliver your children for free. They have had decent training and some of them have a little experience delivering babies. As an added benefit you will have cool stories to tell your surviving children about the adventure.

4. Veterinary rates are typically 50% lower than per hour rates for an M.D. Fundamentally, most procedures and surgeries are pretty much the same. Biology is biology.

How to Save on Travel Expenses

1. Siphon the gas out of your car and put it into your Vespa.

2. Drain the oil from your car and sell it for bus fare.

3. Inflate your tires to get better gas mileage. The president suggests 70 psi. If 70 psi is good, 1000 psi would probably be even better.

4. When you leave for vacation you can save money on having your pet taken care of by dropping him off at the Humane Society. When you get back from your trip, just swing by and pretend you want to adopt him. This will give you a free place to take your pet and he will most likely be vaccinated free of charge...and it works great as long as you don't stay on your trip longer than a week or so.

5. If you're in a faraway city and need a place to stay, you can go to the Y.M.C.A., or you can pick a nice Lexus or Mercedes or other luxury car parked on the street. Use your crow bar to pry open the door. When the alarm goes off pretty soon the police will arrive and the officer will pick you up. For a while you will get pretty decent food and lodging at no cost.

Ways to Save on Groceries

1. Save coupons. Save every coupon you can get your hands on. Never mind that you don't have enough money to buy even one of the products so you can qualify for the two for one. Save the coupons and as you get enough of them you can put them into a sauce pan, add a couple of eggs, cream and sugar, nutmeg, and cook in the oven at 400 degrees for thirty minutes. This recipe sounds to us like it would taste better than caviar.

2. While you're at the dentist's office act like you're waiting for an appointment. Distract the receptionist by asking her to go check on your appointment. While she's checking, use your tennis shoe to scoop a couple of fish out of the cool aquarium there. If you're lucky, along with your fish, you might get a shrimp or escargot.

3. Gardening is popular because it can add to your food with very little expense. If you have no experience, locate someone in your neighborhood who has a nice garden. As soon as it gets dark, grab a flashlight and pepper spray and head into the garden and look for the tomatoes, potatoes, corn, broccoli and other foods you like. (You will need the pepper spray both for seasoning your raw veggies and to disable your neighbor's Rotweiler.) This can be a very inexpensive way to garden.

Saving some dough on Household Expenses and Utility Bills

1. Save on all of your toilet paper and paper towel expenses by substituting late notices and overdraft bank statements.

2. Save on laundry detergent: substitute Jell-O or cement mix. As a bonus you will get some new clothes.

3. To reduce your heating bill, add an additional layer of attic insulation made from shredded, leftover,

no-longer-relevant pieces of the Constitution and Bill of Rights, auto warranties, and toilet paper.

4. Instead of spraying spiders or roaches, spread peanut butter on the floor or carpet and cultivate them. As they multiply and become numerous you can sell them for chicken food or as pets.

How to Cut Your Taxes in Half

1. Sell your hot dog stand, publishing business, or medical practice and go get a part-time job in a car wash. In the first week alone you will be shocked at how much lower your taxes will be.

2. Quit your job as a plumber earning $80.00 an hour and get a job in commission sales.

3. Donate all your paychecks to the local animal sanctuary or, if you like people, the Salvation Army. This will give you a 100% tax deduction.

4. You can cut your tax burden altogether if you completely stop earning money.

5. You can save huge amounts on sales taxes if you stop buying food, clothing, and other consumer items.

You can completely get rid of your tax burden if you sell your business and your land for a fraction of what you paid for them and donate the money to me.

"Take care of your pennies and the dollars will take care of the foreigners and CEOs who run the companies to whom you pay all of your money."

8 The New financial Rules

So many of the traditional rules in this old world are changing. Rules of marriage, rules of appropriate manners, even rules of Monopoly are unrecognizable to some of us older people. I, for one, have been as confused as a grandpa in an electronics store, as nervous as a grasshopper in a chicken coop, and as successful as a European invading Asia.

Fortunately, I have some ideas that can make your financial plans as effective as a skunk in an elevator, as happy as a dung beetle at a political convention, or a school teacher in July. To help you be at peace with the world and function in the economic world as it currently is, here are the changes to the financial rules that have occurred over the past few years. Most of you should commit these to memory. (This will help you stay sane enough that you won't wind up committed to the state nut house, starting a publishing business, or running for Congress.)

Old school Financial Rules

(The ones your grandpa taught you. The ones you thought would always work, but are no longer relevant)

Rule 1: Be honest

Rule 2: Work hard

Rule 3: Stay out of debt

Rule 4: Save as much as you can

Rule 5: Your word is your bond

The New Rules of Finance

(Effective immediately...)

Rule 1: Buy the biggest house you can get.

Rule 2: Save some money if you want to but only after you have everything you want.

Rule 3: Relax; it's the government's job to stimulate the economy.

Rule 4 Always look good.

Rule 5: Your employer probably won't mind if you stay in touch with your chums on Facebook during work hours because, after all, you have a life; besides, it's just work and it's OK to take small stuff from the office and give it to your friends on the days you get to work on time.

Rule 6: What word

As you can see, the changes are significant. If you are one who is still trying to operate under the old system, your life is bound to be confusing.

"Trying to spend or borrow your way out of financial trouble is like trying to stop the bleeding by licking a razor blade... unless you're the government."

9 The History of Poverty as We Know It

The Beginning Years

Like most trendy things in this world, poverty had its humble beginnings in a small town in France. In the early 1400's, a young lady named Joan d' Boat was driving her wooden-wheeled ox cart to town to pick up a sack of rutabagas when a young man named Wesley who was also driving his wooden-wheeled ox cart hauling a load of turnips forgot to look in his mirrors and backed into her, causing approximately $2000 in damage to the frame. Fortunately for Joan a lawyer from the prestigious firm, Bark and Howell, happened by at the precise moment and witnessed everything. He offered to represent her against Wesley's insurance

The Joy of Being Broke

company for a percentage. The case wound up going to court where Joan's lawyer used a never before tried tactic of trying to gain the jury's sympathy. In order to do this, he emphasized her poverty and made her seem even more wretched than she was already. Prior to that moment in court, it had never occurred to Joan that she was poor...wretched, yes, lice-infested, yes, but never poor because she knew she had her health and some loyal friends or "amigos" as they say in France. She also had a spiritual experience in which she received an epiphany that you can get lots of cool stuff given to you if you can get people to feel sorry for you. Being wretched and feeling sorry for yourself pays according to most common apparitions and poltergeists.

Joan's case made the national news and launched her into a career in entertainment where she starred in a whole series of medieval battle films and video games and was eventually burned at the stake after which she went on to arguably the most successful posthumous career in history. Many French concluded that if she could parlay a wretched life of poverty into commercial success and fame, they could, too.

Thanks to this pioneering work in poverty by Joan du Boat, fashionable, profitable oppression and poverty was begun. This breakthrough was followed in rapid succession by the French Revolution, the Estates General, The Roundheads, the Irish potato famine, and eventually Pancho Villa, thereby making possible all kinds of pathetic wretchedness and successful misery. Even Karl Marks got into the act garnering weeks of wall to wall cable news coverage from scandal when he confessed that he really wasn't a communist; he was just goofing around in philosophy class and he thought the word, "proletariat" was really cool. Proletariat, proletariat, proletariat. You should try it.

The Present Years

Which brings us right up to the present time when lots of formerly middle class people suddenly lost half their 401-K's and became suddenly poor or even worse, panicked and sold their 401-K and put what was left into nematode futures, watched their real estate business go to zero and got laid off from their job as a septic tank installer. And so we're wondering what will happen next as our government mortgages our children's future to bail out their friends and change America from home of the brave and land of the free to something else more along the lines of France. We hope it all works out.

My guess is that you probably have some aspect of your life that is wretched and pathetic and so you are probably sitting on a gold mine just like Joan du Boat only hopefully without the burning at the stake. This would probably be a good time to make your own history and do something significant to get us out of this mess or if you are reading this a few years down the road, get us out of this next mess, which we haven't heard of yet. Thank you.

"California 'deer' or 'elk' in prehistoric times were important sources of protein, income, and wealth. Now-a-days they are becoming rare due to rapidly declining habitat being replaced by condos and wilderness."

10 Assets that have No Monetary Value

Some people are obsessed with things they own. They are deluded into believing they are worth way more than they really are. You are most likely one of these. Give it up. You will never get any value for those treasures of yours.

To help you deal with reality, we have compiled this list of your assets that have no monetary value to anyone other than yourself. And let's be honest. If you sell them to yourself, you just get tax liability without any increase in money like small business owners.

Things That Have No Monetary Value

Equities/Securities:

1. Certificates of completion of your defensive driver course.

2. The stock of your BB gun.

3. Certificates of completion of your grand-daughter's pre-school

4. James Bond video tapes in your collection

Precious Metals:

1. The mercury in the fish you caught.

2. The lead in your rear end.

3. The minerals in your tap water.

Art & Collectibles

1. The booger art on the floor of your pickup.

2. Your alcohol-saturated liver.

3. Your deciduous teeth from when you were a kid.

4. Your lymph node collection.

5. Your toddler-finger-stained windows.

6. The imprint of your face on the dash-board of your 1983 Toyota.

7. Your complete collection of tax returns dating back to 1867.

8. Your complete set of traffic citations including a rare traveling below the allowable minimum speed on an expressway.

9. The food in your fridge with expired dates on the labels.

10. Your tattoos of old lovers names on your lower back

11. Any Enron Tattoo no matter where it is on your body

12. Tattoos in general

Intellectual Property:

1. Your twisted sense of humor.

2. Your neurosis.

3. Your insecurity.

4. Your sense of irony.

5. That place you go in your head whenever your kids throw-up.

Real Estate:

1. The pebbles and sand in your tennies.

2. The dirt on your collar.

3. The lint in your belly button.

4. The skids in your kids' underwear.

Livestock:

1. The skunk on the grill of your station wagon.

2. The bird on the grill of your pickup truck.

3. Your breeding pair of house flies.

4. Your taxidermied gopher.

5. Your neighbor's neutered cat.

"Often, the best place to invest your money is in a rainy day reserve of cellulite carried securely on your thighs or belly where you know it will be safe."

11 Fun Things To Do Instead of Knocking Yourself Out Working

Let's be honest. Believing in yourself, getting yourself organized, and going for your dreams of success working night and day, is a lot of trouble. It can cut into your sleep, cause stress and worry, and most important, cut into the time you have for truly important things like video games, interacting with others on the Internet, and hanging out with your friends. Unless you have really thought things through and this is how you want to spend your life, I wouldn't do it.

There was a time in America when a person was expected to knock him or herself out working for success, which required most of us to work harder than a duck going up a waterfall, harder than a snake at a large bird convention, even harder than a hamster in a swamp cooler. Now-a-days, not only is success a real long shot and much tougher than it was in grandpa's day, but over the years, one by one, people have poked their heads up from their wretched lives of toil and strife and noticed that every day more people are sitting on the sidelines watching the handful of dolts who, for what ever reason, still work like beavers damming a fire hose. If you are one who is self-conscious knowing that you are the butt of everybody's jokes because you are a go-getter, but still because of your upbringing, age, or some other handicap, are having a hard time coming up with something else meaningful to do. We present the following.

A List of Fun things to do Instead of Knocking Yourself Out Working for Success

1. Watching reality TV while waiting for your stimulus check.

2. Complaining that you aren't sleeping at night because you doze all day.

3. Dragging your cat on a rope through the alligator swamp.

4. Working to get the image of number 3 out of your mind.

5. Responding apologetically to all the

angry mail you get from sensitive
people who struggle to get the image of
number 3 out of their minds.

6. Running for political office.

7. Parading around the world apolo-
gizing to every third-world
gangster-dictator for all the things
America is.

8. Rallying for trendy left-wing political causes and demanding that someone
else pay for the goodies.

9. Complaining that because you're an
Irish Catholic, Jew, African American,
Hispanic, Woman, Asian, Gay, Mormon,
Asian Mormon Hispanic Woman, Gay
Moslem Irish Catholic Asian, American
Indian Born-again Christian Irish
Catholic Hispanic Woman, African
American Moslem Born Again Christian
Atheist Poor Person, that all the cards in
the deck are stacked against you and
you need monetary compensation to
even things up because of all the preju-
dice and disadvantages your ancestors
suffered hundreds of years ago.

10. Sharpening your self-pity communication skills by calling your congresspersons and whining about all your troubles to try to get them to spend some of your grandchildren's' money on you.

People You Know Who are Also Broke

1. Your Stock Broker

2. Your friends

3. Your banker

4. The author of this book

5. The publisher of this book

6. The distributors of this book

7. Van Gogh

8. Your long lost aunt and uncle

9. Saddam Hussein

10. Somalia

11. Napoleon

12. They guy who grows your food

13. Transistor radio manufacturers

14. Your fairy godmother

15. Sponge Bob

16. Monks

17. Your mechanic

18. Your dog

19. Most farm animals

20. Tiny Tim

21. The people who owned the Titanic

22. Maybe not. Maybe it's the company who insured the Titanic that's broke. Rest assured; somebody in that deal has to be broke.

23. California

"Pictured here is a white Dahl Sheep in a blinding snowstorm or 'snowjob'. Just as a large blizzard can cause the sheep to disappear, a congressional snowjob can help relieve you of your unwanted money."

12 Bad Economic Choices

Some people have to learn the hard way about everything. Fortunately, there are a few who can actually learn from other peoples' bad mistakes and avoid the pain themselves. In case you happen to be one who has this useful life skill, we offer you a bunch of other miserable peoples' poor economic choices. When it comes to losing money and being broke and pathetic, of course the standard ways like losing your job or getting a divorced are usually effective. Here are a few ways you may not have thought of:

Bad Choices - Don't Do These Things

1. Max I. Mum of Septic Springs, Idaho

borrowed $10,000 from his brother-in-law to start a dead cat art brokerage and taxidermist.

2. Stan Dupp of Sheep dip, Montana started a worm farm, then to save money he went out into the swamp to get his own wild worms. These turned out to be water moccasins, which left him with considerable liability.

3. Ben Goode mortgaged his soul to start a book publishing business in his old age.

4. Terry Yaki of Rio Septico, California started a chain of theme-park nursing homes, which might look OK on the surface, but unfortunately she chose as themes Detroit, Subterranean wildlife, and hip-hop/disco.

5. Ann Emic of Methane Falls, Oregon chose to marry a really good looking guy who had no job, future, or money, and who was wanted by the law in five states.

6. Don Key of San Pollo, New Mexico put his bank account number out on the internet asking generous people to put

money into it. This proved to be a bad idea.

More Quick Ways to Become Broke

1. Filling up the gas tank in your pick up truck

2. Starting a small publishing business

3. Going to the doctor or hospital

4. Doing a few gall-bladder surgeries or knee replacements when all the training you have is a high school diploma or the equivalent.

5. Putting your savings into high-yielding sub-prime mortgages

6. Starting up a restaurant serving Brussels sprouts cobbler, and sushi caviar pops.

7. Putting your savings into high-yielding nematode futures.

8. Buying lotto tickets by the thousands on margin.

9. Investing your savings into high-yielding black jack games or roulette.

10. Investing in high quality investment-grade mucous.

11. Investing in a documentary on global whining and bed-wetting.

12. Teaching in the public schools.

13. Starting a hamster tattooing and rodent body piercing business.

14. Funding the research into the development of a new species of toenail fungus.

15. Being the lawyer who defends lawsuits against the manufacture of asbestos bedding and radioactive wet suits.

16. Buying a minor league professional croquet team.

17. Making jokes to the IRS agent about your offshore bank accounts.

18. Making jokes to your wife about other girl friends.

19. Investing your savings in new cars.

20. Paying your utility bills.

21. Investing your savings in a mink-covered match business.

22. Walking down the streets of any big city in the world with your life savings hanging out of your pockets at 2:00 a.m.

23. Making your business plans based on the campaign promises of newly elected politicians.

24. Investing in thousands of Darth Tater Idaho T-shirts.

25. Starting a catburger restaurant in your neighborhood.

26. Buying a boat.

27. Buying an airplane.

28. Investing in a highly leveraged commercial phlegm factory.

"Local savages from Speedtrap, Idaho, partic-
ipate in a shocking ritual of cannibalizing
tourists. Natives here are preparing to eat
the brains of what are believed to be two
bureaucrats, a lawyer, and an actor turned
political activist."

When Flakiness, Waffling, & Indecision are Good Things

13

Not long ago, a friend of mine, who we will call Earl because that's his name, was driving his 1989 Dodge Power Wagon through downtown Badger Flats, Wyo. As he approached the only traffic light in town at the intersection of Post Office and Farmer's Market, the green light turned to yellow. He was still far enough out that whether to stop or try to beat the light was no foregone conclusion. His two brain hemispheres began the well-known debate about what to do. His left-brain was pretty sure he could get his front bumper through the crosswalk and into the intersection before the light turned dark red. On the other hand, his right brain was arguing caution and screaming for him to stop now. Foot on. Foot off. Foot on. Foot off. You know the drill.

Not being used to this much brain activity; Earl's body began to lock up. His eyes began to blur and a vision of his old teddy bear back home began to materialize in the air above his forehead. He was fast losing his ability to do anything rational. The intersection got closer and closer, and the light got pinker and pinker. As luck would have it, events occurred which made the debate a mute point.

Just at the last possible instant, Mildred Flummox's scraggly cat, Fluffy, stepped off the sidewalk and into the street. The sight of her strutting into the intersection jolted Earl back into reality. Since he instinctively knew there was no time to pull his 30-06 down from the gun rack, load it, and fire before Fluffy got back behind some cover, he did the only thing he could think of: he stomped on the gas. He sensed that with a little luck he could get his right, front snow tire onto some portion of the cat before it could scramble into the sewer drain. And so forgetting all about the traffic light, he cranked the wheel with all his might.

With a gallon or so of adrenaline now rushing through his body, Earl failed to notice Sheriff deputy Frank Foote standing on the corner chatting with this very same Mildred Flummox until it was too late. His front wheels hit the three-inches of water that had sat for decades in a puddle by the curb and splashed a couple gallons of it all over officer Frank and Mildred just an instant before the same right snow tire that was aiming for Fluffy bounced off the curb at a bad angle and sailed onto the sidewalk landing squarely onto Officer Frank's now wet metacarpals. Fluffy adjusted her direction quick as a cat and escaped into the storm drain all 9 lives still intact. Earl's pickup truck came to a stop with its bumper ground into the wall of Rick Farrer's septic pumping and tax preparation office, right next to the spot where Mildred and Deputy Frank had been standing before Mildred leaped through the picture window of Thomas Hebron's soda fountain. The power Wagon wheels settled on top of Deputy Frank's now empty boots.

After that moment, now frozen in time in Earl's mind, things pretty much happened like you would expect. And so we see that if Earl had only remained in a frozen state of indecision, he would have most likely received nothing worse than the hairy eyeball from Officer Frank and Mildred, cautioning him to slow down and not be in such an all fired hurry, instead of having both his auto and health insurance rates double because of the auto and hospital claims submitted after Officer Frank smashed all the windows and mirrors in Earl's truck with his night stick and Earl was laid up with kidney problems from taking pain medication and eating hospital food while his bones knitted back together.

Just like in Earl's life, when it comes to our finances, indecision can sometimes be our friend. Over the years I have observed that most of the people in my life who are decisive with their finances, and who go forward with confidence and optimism to invest in that dream of theirs, the iguana farm or the bat guano recycling station or booger-humor publishing business, wind up borrowing money, often from the very same people who were frozen in indecision and couldn't make up their minds to invest their money until their once-in-a-life-time opportunity had passed to try to keep from losing their house after their venture turned to compost. So if you're one of those who always seem to miss out on all the fantastic opportunities because of indecision, don't be too hard on yourself. Although you may not have your bat guano recycling business, at least you probably still have your money. And that should count for something.

Some Random Ways to Tell if an Investment is a Bad Idea

1. Yes, it is most likely a bad idea.
2. I wouldn't do it if I were you.
3. If you can't afford to lose all your money plus be saddled with debt for the next forty years and have everyone you know hate you and think you're a crook, don't do it.
4. You have rotten luck.
5. If you are involved in any material way, it's inevitable that things will go south.
6. It's a can't fail-sure thing.

A Few Random Ways to Tell if an Investment is a Good Idea

1. Nobody you know has anything to do with it.

2. You are pretty sure it's a bad idea.
3. It doesn't cost you anything or require that you do anything at all.
4. You ponder the water too long and miss your chance to get involved.
5. You are forced to pass on it because you don't have the time or money.
6. You think it looks illegal.

"Male mule deer become extremely aggressive during mating season and tax time. The buck pictured here was caught on camera just as he smashed his head clear through the wall."

14 Questions & Answers

Q. My rich uncle just died leaving me $fifteen billion in cash, four Bavarian castles, and his cat, Frisky. I have been among the wretched poor all my life. I don't know what to do.

A. Drop the cat off at the humane society on your way to my office. Meanwhile, don't take any phone calls or talk to anyone until you get here. If you need something to do on the way, read chapters one and six of my book. Did I mention that I am the best financial counselor I personally know?

The Joy of Being Broke

Q. My friend and I are arguing whether poverty is a learned skill or genetic. I say it's genetic because I was born broke and after all these years am still pathetic. Could you settle this for us?

A. Having never met you, I have no idea whether or not you are a goofball, but I know that financial problems are mostly genetic. They found a chemical in my blood stream that causes me to spend more than I make and borrow money at outrageous interest rates. They're currently working on a medication for the condition. Meanwhile, I've chosen to have a creditcardobotomy and am in need of some serious sympathy.

Q. Since I recently lost my business, my retirement, house, cars, self-respect and health, my dog, Sparky, and I are sharing the remnants of a sack of Kibbles and Bits. We plan to augment this with good nutrition we find dumpster diving. Do you know a good vitamin supplement to help us balance nutrition with healthy weight loss and intestinal parasites?

A. If you still have your computer you can find some info on line at www.dumpsterhealth.gov. Also, rather than maliciously killing your parasites (tapeworms are people, too.) try turning them into pets. Just be aware that these particular pets can sometimes affect your social life.

Q. Since I lost everything, I've been thoroughly enjoying my poverty; however, my wife doesn't seem to be as into it as I am. Is there anything I can do to make her happier living in squalor?

A. Yes, of course, there is a strategy that works with every woman fixing nearly every kind of problem. Just sidle up to her, look her in the eyes and tell her, sincerely, "Honey, I just put $10,000 into your bank account."

Q. Back when I was a millionaire jet setter, I used to be able to get lots of women, even though I'm an unattractive dweebe. I always just bought them lots of cool stuff and gave them money before. How do broke guys get women?

A. Most turn to celibacy and many have pets.

Q. The wife and I have always been quite content being broke and wretched. Lately, for some reason, feelings are awakening that are causing us to change. I am starting to feel like I want to start my own business and we are getting pretty excited about investing in a worm farm. Do you think this is a good idea?

A. Look at the statistics. The odds against you succeeding in your own little business are worse than the odds of your chicken outrunning your camel; worse than the odds of your congressperson voting herself a pay cut. Better stick to something for which you have some aptitude and a realistic chance of success. Being broke is something you know you can do. Why not hang with it?

On the other hand, if you, like millions of other brain-damaged souls, are determined to try your own small business, despite inevitable failure and misery, public humiliation, my dire warnings, and possibly even death by regulatory strangulation, at least find a business where you won't have to pay FICA, workers comp. Medicare, Medicaid, state taxes, licensing, employee health insurance, and so forth and that won't require that you try to collect on invoices from other struggling businesses. And if you can, find one that pays you benefits and gives you a car.

Q. I am in jail. When I get out do I still get to be broke?

A. More than anything, being broke is an attitude. Can you whine? Can you blame others for your failures? Can you feel sorry for yourself? If you can, and jail is a great place to learn these skills, you've got a bright future.

Q. Since I lost half my income and can no longer pay my bills, the bank has repossessed my car, which is how I get to work at the Goebbels Turkey Plucking Foundry, which is how I used to pay my bills. Since the banks used taxpayer money to bail themselves out when they got into trouble, shouldn't they cut us taxpayers a little slack/ since we didn't get bailed out?

A. The government feels that since you have government sponsored school lunch and the Salvation Army, that should be bailout enough for those of you who have little money and only one vote. When you get your stimulus check, consider it your bailout. You are a small person; so naturally, your bailout is also small.

Q. I've got along pretty well financially for my entire life until recently when I've become quite poor. I'm having a hard time adjusting. Can you make any recommendations?

A. A wise guy once told me, "Dude! With all the talent and smarts you possess, and with this bunch in charge, you should probably lower your expectations." I've found this to be good advice.

Q. I have been told I'm not very bright, that I'm lazy and my life is going nowhere. I'm also very poor and have questionable morals. What would you think about a career in Congress?

A. Before a person of your ilk should consider a career in Congress, you need to do some research and find out what is the current going price for a previously un-sold soul. Do your research early because if what you tell me is true, the minute word gets out that you want to run, one of the political parties will be all over you.

Q. I owe back taxes, am delinquent on my mortgage and credit cards, my car is broke down and I can't afford to fix it. Does this mean I'm broke?

A. Yes.

Q. I am a very wealthy person considering adopting the broke lifestyle. If I become broke and pathetic can I still order pizza and keep my spa membership?

A. The government considers both pizza and spa memberships essential goods and services and thus, they are covered under section 666 of the welfare code.

'The Truth About Life' Humor Books

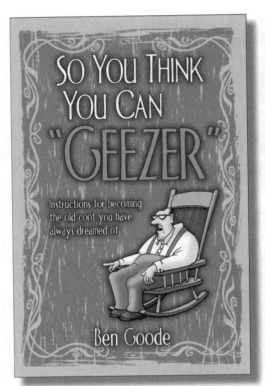

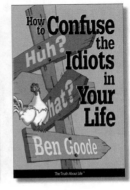

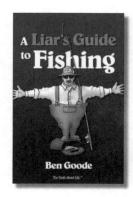
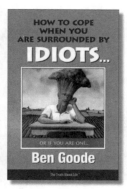
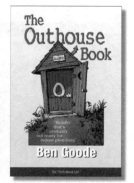

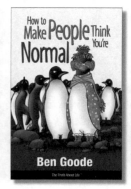
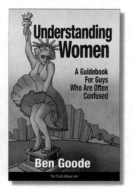

Apricot Press Order Form

Book Title	Quantity	x	Cost / Book	=	Total
_____	_____	_____	_____		_____
_____	_____	_____	_____		_____
_____	_____	_____	_____		_____
_____	_____	_____	_____		_____
_____	_____	_____	_____		_____
_____	_____	_____	_____		_____
_____	_____	_____	_____		_____
_____	_____	_____	_____		_____

All Humor Books are $6.95 US.   **All Cook Books are $9.95 US.**

Do not send Cash. Mail check or money order to:
**Apricot Press   P.O. Box 98
Nephi, Utah   84648**
Telephone 435-623-1929
Allow 3 weeks for delivery.

**Quantity discounts available.
Call us for more information.**
9 a.m. - 5 p.m. MST

Sub Total = _____

Shipping = **$2.00**

Tax 8.5% = _____

Total Amount
Enclosed = _____

Shipping Address

Name: _____

Street: _____

City: _____   State: _____

Zip Code: _____

Telephone: _____

Email: _____